GRATITUDE JOURNAL

GRATITUDE JOURNAL

A Gratitude Journal is a record of things for which one is grateful. It makes you focus your attention on the positive things in your life. Gratitude is strongly associated with greater happiness.

We all have the ability and opportunity to practice gratitude. Start a routine of writing things you are grateful for in this journal and watch your life change.

Happiness depends upon ourselves. - Aristotle

A single grateful thought toward heaven is the most perfect prayer.

– Gotthold Ephraim Lessing

Day: ______________ *Date:* ___/___/___

Today I am *Grateful* for ______________________________

He who is not contented with what he has, would not be contented with what he would like to have. - Socrates

Day: ______________ *Date:* ___/___/___

Today I am *Grateful* for ______________________________

Day: ______________ *Date:* ___/___/___

Today I am *Grateful* for ______________________

If you hope for happiness in the world, hope for it from God, and not from the world.
- David Brainerd

Day: ______________ *Date:* ___/___/___

Today I am *Grateful* for ______________________

Day: ______________ *Date:* ___/___/___

Today I am *Grateful* for ______________________________

Be happy with what you have and are, be generous with both, and you won't have to hunt for happiness. - *William E. Gladstone*

Day: ______________ *Date:* ___/___/___

Today I am *Grateful* for ______________________________

Day: ______________ *Date:* ___/___/___

Today I am *Grateful* for ______________________________

____

____

____

____

____

____

Let us be grateful to people who make us happy, they are the charming gardeners who make our souls blossom. - Marcel Proust

Day: ______________ *Date:* ___/___/___

Today I am *Grateful* for ______________________________

____

____

____

____

____

____

Day: ______________ *Date:* ___/___/___

Today I am *Grateful* for ______________________________

Happiness... consists in giving, and in serving others. - Henry Drummond

Day: ______________ *Date:* ___/___/___

Today I am *Grateful* for ______________________________

Day: ______________ *Date:* ___/___/___

Today I am *Grateful* for ______________________________

____

____

____

____

____

Gratitude is not only the greatest of virtues, but the parent of all the others.
- Marcus Tullius Cicero

Day: ______________ *Date:* ___/___/___

Today I am *Grateful* for ______________________________

____

____

____

____

____

Day: ______________ *Date:* ___/___/___

Today I am *Grateful* for ______________________________

Well done is better than well said. - Benjamin Franklin

Day: ______________ *Date:* ___/___/___

Today I am *Grateful* for ______________________________

Day: ______________ *Date:* ___/___/___

Today I am *Grateful* for

Our happiness depends on wisdom all the way. - Sophocles

Day: ______________ *Date:* ___/___/___

Today I am *Grateful* for

Day: ______________ *Date:* ___/___/___

Today I am *Grateful* for ______________________________

Hope smiles from the threshold of the year to come, whispering, 'It will be happier.'
- Alfred Lord Tennyson

Day: ______________ *Date:* ___/___/___

Today I am *Grateful* for ______________________________

Day: ______________ *Date:* ___/___/___

Today I am *Grateful* for ____________________

____

____

____

____

____

____

Appreciation is a wonderful thing: It makes what is excellent in others belong to us as well. - Voltaire

Day: ______________ *Date:* ___/___/___

Today I am *Grateful* for ____________________

____

____

____

____

____

____

Day: _______________ *Date:* ____/____/____

Today I am *Grateful* for ________________________________

____

____

____

____

____

____

When unhappy, one doubts everything; when happy, one doubts nothing. - Joseph Roux

Day: _______________ *Date:* ____/____/____

Today I am *Grateful* for ________________________________

____

____

____

____

____

____

Day: ____________ *Date:* ___/___/___

Today I am *Grateful* for

Nothing is so contagious as enthusiasm. - Samuel Taylor Coleridge

Day: ____________ *Date:* ___/___/___

Today I am *Grateful* for

Day: ______________ *Date:* ___/___/___

Today I am *Grateful* for ____________________________________

____

____

____

____

____

____

The essence of all beautiful art, all great art, is gratitude. - Friedrich Nietzsche

Day: ______________ *Date:* ___/___/___

Today I am *Grateful* for ____________________________________

____

____

____

____

____

____

Day: ________________ *Date:* ____/____/____

Today I am *Grateful* for ______________________________

____

____

____

____

____

____

God has two dwellings; one in heaven, and the other in a meek and thankful heart.
- Izaak Walton

Day: ________________ *Date:* ____/____/____

Today I am *Grateful* for ______________________________

____

____

____

____

____

____

Day: ______________ *Date:* ___/___/___

Today I am *Grateful* for ______________________________

____

____

____

____

____

Saying thank you is more than good manners. It is good spirituality. - Alfred Agache

Day: ______________ *Date:* ___/___/___

Today I am *Grateful* for ______________________________

____

____

____

____

____

Day: ____________ *Date:* ___/___/___

Today I am *Grateful* for

The most certain sign of wisdom is cheerfulness. - Michel de Montaigne

Day: ____________ *Date:* ___/___/___

Today I am *Grateful* for

Day: ____________ *Date:* ___/___/___

Today I am *Grateful* for ______________________

Courtesies of a small and trivial character are the ones which strike deepest in the grateful and appreciating heart. - Henry Clay

Day: ____________ *Date:* ___/___/___

Today I am *Grateful* for ______________________

Day: ____________ *Date:* ___/___/___

Today I am *Grateful* for ______________________

____

____

____

____

____

____

To keep the heart unwrinkled, to be hopeful, kindly, cheerful, reverent that is to triumph over old age. - Amos Bronson Alcott

Day: ____________ *Date:* ___/___/___

Today I am *Grateful* for ______________________

____

____

____

____

____

____

Day: ____________ *Date:* ___/___/___

Today I am *Grateful* for ____________________

____

____

____

____

____

____

There is only one thing that can form a bond between men, and that is gratitude… we cannot give someone else greater power over us than we have ourselves. - Charles de Secondat

Day: ____________ *Date:* ___/___/___

Today I am *Grateful* for ____________________

____

____

____

____

____

____

Day: ____________ *Date:* ___/___/___

Today I am *Grateful* for ______________________________

The art of being happy lies in the power of extracting happiness from common things.
- Henry Ward Beecher

Day: ____________ *Date:* ___/___/___

Today I am *Grateful* for ______________________________

Day: ____________ *Date:* ___/___/___

Today I am *Grateful* for ____________

Cheerfulness is the best promoter of health and is as friendly to the mind as to the body.
- Joseph Addison

Day: ____________ *Date:* ___/___/___

Today I am *Grateful* for ____________

Day: ________________ *Date:* ____/____/____

Today I am *Grateful* for

Energy and persistence conquer all things. *Benjamin Franklin*

Day: ________________ *Date:* ____/____/____

Today I am *Grateful* for

Day: ____________ *Date:* ___/___/___

Today I am *Grateful* for ____________________

Gratitude is the sign of noble souls. - Aesop Fables

Day: ____________ *Date:* ___/___/___

Today I am *Grateful* for ____________________

Day: ______________ *Date:* ___/___/___

Today I am *Grateful* for ______________________________

There is nothing on this earth more to be prized than true friendship. -Thomas Aquinas

Day: ______________ *Date:* ___/___/___

Today I am *Grateful* for ______________________________

Day: ____________ *Date:* ___/___/___

Today I am *Grateful* for ______________________

____

____

____

____

____

____

Truly, it is in darkness that one finds the light, so when we are in sorrow, then this light is nearest of all to us. - Meister Eckhart

Day: ____________ *Date:* ___/___/___

Today I am *Grateful* for ______________________

____

____

____

____

____

____

Day: ______________ *Date:* ___/___/___

Today I am *Grateful* for ______________

There is only one way to happiness and that is to cease worrying about things which are beyond the power of our will. - Epictetus

Day: ______________ *Date:* ___/___/___

Today I am *Grateful* for ______________

Day: ____________ *Date:* ___/___/___

Today I am *Grateful* for ______________________________

That man is a success who has lived well, laughed often and loved much.
- Robert Louis Stevenson

Day: ____________ *Date:* ___/___/___

Today I am *Grateful* for ______________________________

Day: ______________ *Date:* ___/___/___

Today I am *Grateful* for ______________________________

____

____

____

____

____

____

True life is lived when tiny changes occur. - Leo Tolstoy

Day: ______________ *Date:* ___/___/___

Today I am *Grateful* for ______________________________

____

____

____

____

____

____

Day: ______________ *Date:* ___/___/___

Today I am *Grateful* for ______________________________

When I let go of what I am, I become what I might be. - Lao Tzu

Day: ______________ *Date:* ___/___/___

Today I am *Grateful* for ______________________________

Day: ______________ *Date:* ___/___/___

Today I am *Grateful* for ______________________________

____

____

____

____

____

____

If we learn not humility, we learn nothing. - John Jewel

Day: ______________ *Date:* ___/___/___

Today I am *Grateful* for ______________________________

____

____

____

____

____

____

Day: ______________ *Date:* ___/___/___

Today I am *Grateful* for

If the only prayer you ever say in your entire life is thank you, it will be enough.
- Meister Eckhart

Day: ______________ *Date:* ___/___/___

Today I am *Grateful* for

Day: ______________ *Date:* ___/___/___

Today I am *Grateful* for

Three things cannot be long hidden: the sun, the moon, and the truth. - Buddha

Day: ______________ *Date:* ___/___/___

Today I am *Grateful* for

Day: ____________ *Date:* ___/___/___

Today I am *Grateful* for ____________

A man who fears suffering is already suffering from what he fears.
- Michel de Montaigne

Day: ____________ *Date:* ___/___/___

Today I am *Grateful* for ____________

Day: ____________ *Date:* ___/___/___

Today I am *Grateful* for ______________________

____

____

____

____

____

____

Character is the result of two things: mental attitude and the way we spend our time.
- Elbert Hubbard

Day: ____________ *Date:* ___/___/___

Today I am *Grateful* for ______________________

____

____

____

____

____

____

Day: ______________ *Date:* ___/___/___

Today I am *Grateful* for ______________________________

Correction does much, but encouragement does more. - Johann Wolfgang von Goethe

Day: ______________ *Date:* ___/___/___

Today I am *Grateful* for ______________________________

Day: ______________ *Date:* ___/___/___

Today I am *Grateful* for ______________________________

Conscience is a man's compass. - Vincent Van Gogh

Day: ______________ *Date:* ___/___/___

Today I am *Grateful* for ______________________________

Day: ____________ *Date:* ___/___/___

Today I am *Grateful* for ________________________

Compared to what we ought to be, we are half awake. - William James

Day: ____________ *Date:* ___/___/___

Today I am *Grateful* for ________________________

Day: ______________ *Date:* ___/___/___

Today I am *Grateful* for

Silence is a source of great strength. Lao Tzu

Day: ______________ *Date:* ___/___/___

Today I am *Grateful* for

Day: ____________ *Date:* ___/___/___

Today I am *Grateful* for ________________________

Curiosity is one of the most permanent and certain characteristics of a vigorous intellect.
- Samuel Johnson

Day: ____________ *Date:* ___/___/___

Today I am *Grateful* for ________________________

Day: ____________ *Date:* ___/___/___

Today I am *Grateful* for

It is not length of life, but depth of life. - Ralph Waldo Emerson

Day: ____________ *Date:* ___/___/___

Today I am *Grateful* for

Day: __________ *Date:* ___/___/___

Today I am *Grateful* for

Faith is a knowledge within the heart, beyond the reach of proof. - Khalil Gibran

Day: __________ *Date:* ___/___/___

Today I am *Grateful* for

Day: ______________ *Date:* ___/___/___

Today I am *Grateful* for ______________________________

If you think you can win, you can win. Faith is necessary to victory. - William Hazlitt

Day: ______________ *Date:* ___/___/___

Today I am *Grateful* for ______________________________

Day: ____________ *Date:* ___/___/___

Today I am *Grateful* for ____________________

____

____

____

____

____

____

The eye sees what it brings the power to see. - Thomas Carlyle

Day: ____________ *Date:* ___/___/___

Today I am *Grateful* for ____________________

____

____

____

____

____

____

Day: ______________ *Date:* ___/___/___

Today I am *Grateful* for ______________________________

The earth laughs in flowers. - Ralph Waldo Emerson

Day: ______________ *Date:* ___/___/___

Today I am *Grateful* for ______________________________

Day: __________ *Date:* ___/___/___

Today I am *Grateful* for

To err is human; to forgive, divine. - Alexander Pope

Day: __________ *Date:* ___/___/___

Today I am *Grateful* for

Day: ______________ *Date:* ___/___/___

Today I am *Grateful* for ______________________________

Life's like a play: it's not the length, but the excellence of the acting that matters.
- Lucius Annaeus Seneca

Day: ______________ *Date:* ___/___/___

Today I am *Grateful* for ______________________________

Day: ______________ *Date:* ___/___/___

Today I am *Grateful* for ______________

Friends are the siblings God never gave us. - Mencius

Day: ______________ *Date:* ___/___/___

Today I am *Grateful* for ______________

Day: ____________ *Date:* ___/___/___

Today I am *Grateful* for ____________________

The greatest discovery of my generation is that a human being can alter his life by altering his attitudes. - William James

Day: ____________ *Date:* ___/___/___

Today I am *Grateful* for ____________________

Day: _______________ *Date:* ___/___/___

Today I am *Grateful* for ________________________________

____

____

____

____

____

____

Be glad of life because it gives you the chance to love, to work, to play, and to look up at the stars. - Henry Van Dyke

Day: _______________ *Date:* ___/___/___

Today I am *Grateful* for ________________________________

____

____

____

____

____

____

Day: __________ *Date:* ___/___/___

Today I am *Grateful* for

Do not consider painful what is good for you. - Euripides

Day: __________ *Date:* ___/___/___

Today I am *Grateful* for

Day: ____________ *Date:* ___/___/___

Today I am *Grateful* for ____________

Patience and time do more than strength or passion. - Jean de La Fontaine

Day: ____________ *Date:* ___/___/___

Today I am *Grateful* for ____________

Day: ______________ *Date:* ____/____/____

Today I am *Grateful* for ______________________________

The soul never thinks without a picture. - Aristotle

Day: ______________ *Date:* ____/____/____

Today I am *Grateful* for ______________________________

Day: ________________ *Date:* ___/___/___

Today I am *Grateful* for ______________________________

____

____

____

____

____

____

Next to acquiring good friends, the best acquisition is that of good books.
- Charles Caleb Colton

Day: ________________ *Date:* ___/___/___

Today I am *Grateful* for ______________________________

____

____

____

____

____

____

Day: ______________ *Date:* ___/___/___

Today I am *Grateful* for ______________________________

____

____

____

____

____

____

Sincerity is the way to heaven. - Mencius

Day: ______________ *Date:* ___/___/___

Today I am *Grateful* for ______________________________

____

____

____

____

____

____

Day: ____________ *Date:* ___/___/___

Today I am *Grateful* for

Look around for a place to sow a few seeds. - Henry Van Dyke

Day: ____________ *Date:* ___/___/___

Today I am *Grateful* for

Day: ______________ *Date:* ___/___/___

Today I am *Grateful* for ______________________________

____

____

____

____

____

____

Every moment of light and dark is a miracle. - Walt Whitman

Day: ______________ *Date:* ___/___/___

Today I am *Grateful* for ______________________________

____

____

____

____

____

____

Day: ______________ *Date:* ___/___/___

Today I am *Grateful* for ______________________________

____

____

____

____

____

____

Thus happiness depends, as nature shows, less on exterior things than most suppose.
- William Cowper

Day: ______________ *Date:* ___/___/___

Today I am *Grateful* for ______________________________

____

____

____

____

____

____

Day: ______________ *Date:* ___/___/___

Today I am *Grateful* for ______________________________

Never look back unless you are planning to go that way. - Henry David Thoreau

Day: ______________ *Date:* ___/___/___

Today I am *Grateful* for ______________________________

Day: ____________ *Date:* ___/___/___

Today I am *Grateful* for ____________

No blessing lasts forever. - Plautus

Day: ____________ *Date:* ___/___/___

Today I am *Grateful* for ____________

Day: ____________ *Date:* ___/___/___

Today I am *Grateful* for ____________

The heart is forever making the head its fool.- Francois de La Rochefoucauld

Day: ____________ *Date:* ___/___/___

Today I am *Grateful* for ____________

Day: ______________ *Date:* ___/___/___

Today I am *Grateful* for ________________________________

____

____

____

____

____

____

One returns to the place one came from. - Jean de La Fontaine

Day: ______________ *Date:* ___/___/___

Today I am *Grateful* for ________________________________

____

____

____

____

____

____

Day: ______________ *Date:* ___/___/___

Today I am *Grateful* for

The present time has one advantage over every other - it is our own. - Charles Caleb Colton

Day: ______________ *Date:* ___/___/___

Today I am *Grateful* for

Day: ______________ *Date:* ___/___/___

Today I am *Grateful* for ____________________

____

____

____

____

____

____

Laughter is not at all a bad beginning for a friendship, and it is far the best ending for one. - Oscar Wilde

Day: ______________ *Date:* ___/___/___

Today I am *Grateful* for ____________________

____

____

____

____

____

____

Day: ____________ *Date:* ___/___/___

Today I am *Grateful* for

They know enough who know how to learn. - Henry Adams

Day: ____________ *Date:* ___/___/___

Today I am *Grateful* for

Day: ___________ *Date:* ___/___/___

Today I am *Grateful* for

Much wisdom often goes with fewest words. - Sophocles

Day: ___________ *Date:* ___/___/___

Today I am *Grateful* for

Day: ______________ *Date:* ___/___/___

Today I am *Grateful* for ______________________________

The darkest day, if you live till tomorrow, will have passed away.
- William Cowper

Day: ______________ *Date:* ___/___/___

Today I am *Grateful* for ______________________________

Day: ______________ *Date:* ___/___/___

Today I am *Grateful* for ______________________________

____

____

____

____

____

____

A short cut to riches is to subtract from our desires. - Petrarch

Day: ______________ *Date:* ___/___/___

Today I am *Grateful* for ______________________________

____

____

____

____

____

____

Day: ______________ *Date:* ___/___/___

Today I am *Grateful* for ______________________

True life is lived when tiny changes occur.
- Leo Tolstoy

Day: ______________ *Date:* ___/___/___

Today I am *Grateful* for ______________________

Day: ______________ *Date:* ___/___/___

Today I am *Grateful* for ______________________________

____

____

____

____

____

____

Where there are friends there is wealth. - Plautus

Day: ______________ *Date:* ___/___/___

Today I am *Grateful* for ______________________________

____

____

____

____

____

____

Day: ______________ *Date:* ___/___/___

Today I am *Grateful* for ______________________________

____

____

____

____

____

____

You can give without loving, but you can never love without giving. - Robert Louis Stevenson

Day: ______________ *Date:* ___/___/___

Today I am *Grateful* for ______________________________

____

____

____

____

____

____

Day: ______________ *Date:* ___/___/___

Today I am *Grateful* for

To know that we know what we know, and to know that we do not know what we do not know, that is true knowledge. - Nicolaus Copernicus

Day: ______________ *Date:* ___/___/___

Today I am *Grateful* for

Day: ______________ *Date:* ___/___/___

Today I am *Grateful* for ______________________________

____

____

____

____

____

____

Real happiness is cheap enough, yet how dearly we pay for its counterfeit. - Hosea Ballou

Day: ______________ *Date:* ___/___/___

Today I am *Grateful* for ______________________________

____

____

____

____

____

____

Day: ________________ *Date:* ___/___/___

Today I am *Grateful* for ____________________________________

____

____

____

____

____

Adventure is not outside man; it is within. - George Eliot

Day: ________________ *Date:* ___/___/___

Today I am *Grateful* for ____________________________________

____

____

____

____

____

Day: ______________ *Date:* ___/___/___

Today I am *Grateful* for ______________________________

____

____

____

____

____

____

Experience is simply the name we give our mistakes. - Oscar Wilde

Day: ______________ *Date:* ___/___/___

Today I am *Grateful* for ______________________________

____

____

____

____

____

____

Day: ____________ *Date:* ___/___/___

Today I am *Grateful* for ____________

Happiness is a choice that requires effort at times. - Aeschylus

Day: ____________ *Date:* ___/___/___

Today I am *Grateful* for ____________

Day: ______________ *Date:* ___/___/___

Today I am *Grateful* for ______________________________

Always desire to learn something useful. - Sophocles

Day: ______________ *Date:* ___/___/___

Today I am *Grateful* for ______________________________

Day: ______________ *Date:* ___/___/___

Today I am *Grateful* for ______________________________

____

____

____

____

____

To be content with what we possess is the greatest and most secure of riches.
- Marcus Tullius Cicero

Day: ______________ *Date:* ___/___/___

Today I am *Grateful* for ______________________________

____

____

____

____

____

Day: ______________ *Date:* ___/___/___

Today I am *Grateful* for ______________________________

The clearest way into the Universe is through a forest wilderness. - John Muir

Day: ______________ *Date:* ___/___/___

Today I am *Grateful* for ______________________________

Day: ____________ *Date:* ___/___/___

Today I am *Grateful* for ________________

It will never rain roses: when we want to have more roses we must plant more trees.
- George Eliot

Day: ____________ *Date:* ___/___/___

Today I am *Grateful* for ________________

Day: ______________ *Date:* ___/___/___

Today I am *Grateful* for ______________________

____

____

____

____

____

____

When we try to pick out anything by itself, we find it hitched to everything else in the universe. - John Muir

Day: ______________ *Date:* ___/___/___

Today I am *Grateful* for ______________________

____

____

____

____

____

____

Day: ______________ *Date:* ___/___/___

Today I am *Grateful* for ________________________

Hatred is self-punishment. - Hosea Ballou

Day: ______________ *Date:* ___/___/___

Today I am *Grateful* for ________________________

Day: ____________ *Date:* ___/___/___

Today I am *Grateful* for ____________________

Give light, and the darkness will disappear of itself. - Desiderius Erasmus

Day: ____________ *Date:* ___/___/___

Today I am *Grateful* for ____________________

Day: ______________ *Date:* ___/___/___

Today I am *Grateful* for ______________________________

Enthusiasm moves the world. - Arthur Balfour

Day: ______________ *Date:* ___/___/___

Today I am *Grateful* for ______________________________

Day: ______________ *Date:* ___/___/___

Today I am *Grateful* for ______________________________

____

____

____

____

____

____

What is not started today is never finished tomorrow. - Johann Wolfgang von Goethe

Day: ______________ *Date:* ___/___/___

Today I am *Grateful* for ______________________________

____

____

____

____

____

____

Day: ______________ *Date:* ___/___/___

Today I am *Grateful* for ______________________________

We are always getting ready to live but never living. - Ralph Waldo Emerson

Day: ______________ *Date:* ___/___/___

Today I am *Grateful* for ______________________________

Day: ______________ *Date:* ___/___/___

Today I am *Grateful* for ______________________________

Time brings all things to pass. - Aeschylus

Day: ______________ *Date:* ___/___/___

Today I am *Grateful* for ______________________________

Day: ______________ *Date:* ___/___/___

Today I am *Grateful* for ______________________________

High thoughts must have high language. - Aristophanes

Day: ______________ *Date:* ___/___/___

Today I am *Grateful* for ______________________________

Day: ______________ *Date:* ___/___/___

Today I am *Grateful* for ______________________________

____

____

____

____

____

____

To give thanks in solitude is enough. Thanksgiving has wings and goes where it must go. Your prayer knows much more about it than you do. - Victor Hugo

Day: ______________ *Date:* ___/___/___

Today I am *Grateful* for ______________________________

____

____

____

____

____

____

Day: ______________ *Date:* ___/___/___

Today I am *Grateful* for ______________________________

____

____

____

____

____

____

Do exactly what you would do if you felt most secure. - Meister Eckhart

Day: ______________ *Date:* ___/___/___

Today I am *Grateful* for ______________________________

____

____

____

____

____

____

Day: ____________ *Date:* ___/___/___

Today I am *Grateful* for ______________________________

____

____

____

____

____

____

Hope is but the dream of those who wake. - Matthew Prior

Day: ____________ *Date:* ___/___/___

Today I am *Grateful* for ______________________________

____

____

____

____

____

____

Day: ____________ *Date:* ___/___/___

Today I am *Grateful* for ______________________________

Be happy for this moment. This moment is your life. - Omar Khayyam

Day: ____________ *Date:* ___/___/___

Today I am *Grateful* for ______________________________

Day: ______________ *Date:* ___/___/___

Today I am *Grateful* for ______________________________

____

____

____

____

____

____

A lie can travel half way around the world while the truth is putting on its shoes.
- Charles Spurgeon

Day: ______________ *Date:* ___/___/___

Today I am *Grateful* for ______________________________

____

____

____

____

____

____

Day: ____________ *Date:* ___/___/___

Today I am *Grateful* for ____________________

It is the chiefest point of happiness that a man is willing to be what he is.
- Desiderius Erasmus

Day: ____________ *Date:* ___/___/___

Today I am *Grateful* for ____________________

Day: ____________ *Date:* ___/___/___

Today I am *Grateful* for ________________________________

____

____

____

____

____

____

There is only one happiness in this life, to love and be loved. George Sand

Day: ____________ *Date:* ___/___/___

Today I am *Grateful* for ________________________________

____

____

____

____

____

____

Day: ________________ *Date:* ____/____/____

Today I am *Grateful* for ______________________________

____

____

____

____

____

____

Be curious, not judgmental. - Walt Whitman

Day: ________________ *Date:* ____/____/____

Today I am *Grateful* for ______________________________

____

____

____

____

____

____

Day: ______________ *Date:* ___/___/___

Today I am *Grateful* for ______________________________

____

____

____

____

____

____

All money is a matter of belief. Adam Smith

Day: ______________ *Date:* ___/___/___

Today I am *Grateful* for ______________________________

____

____

____

____

____

____

Day: ______________ *Date:* ___/___/___

Today I am *Grateful* for ______________________________

____

____

____

____

____

No one ever became great except through many and great mistakes.
- William E. Gladstone

Day: ______________ *Date:* ___/___/___

Today I am *Grateful* for ______________________________

____

____

____

____

____

Day: ______________ *Date:* ___/___/___

Today I am *Grateful* for ______________________________

Being brilliant is no great feat if you respect nothing. - Johann Wolfgang von Goethe

Day: ______________ *Date:* ___/___/___

Today I am *Grateful* for ______________________________

Day: ____________ *Date:* ___/___/___

Today I am *Grateful* for ____________

There is no happiness in having or in getting, but only in giving. - Henry Drummond

Day: ____________ *Date:* ___/___/___

Today I am *Grateful* for ____________

Day: ____________ *Date:* ___/___/___

Today I am *Grateful* for ________________________

The happiness which is lacking makes one think even the happiness one has unbearable.
- Joseph Roux

Day: ____________ *Date:* ___/___/___

Today I am *Grateful* for ________________________

Day: ______________ *Date:* ___/___/___

Today I am *Grateful* for ______________________

A happy life is one which is in accordance with its own nature. - Lucius Annaeus Seneca

Day: ______________ *Date:* ___/___/___

Today I am *Grateful* for ______________________

Day: ______________ *Date:* ___/___/___

Today I am *Grateful* for ____________________________

Perseverance, secret of all triumphs. - Victor Hugo

Day: ______________ *Date:* ___/___/___

Today I am *Grateful* for ____________________________

Day: ____________ *Date:* ___/___/___

Today I am *Grateful* for ______________________________

The ends must justify the means. - Matthew Prior

Day: ____________ *Date:* ___/___/___

Today I am *Grateful* for ______________________________

Day: ______________ *Date:* ___/___/___

Today I am *Grateful* for ______________________

'Tis better to have loved and lost than never to have loved at all. - Alfred Lord Tennyson

Day: ______________ *Date:* ___/___/___

Today I am *Grateful* for ______________________

Day: ______________ *Date:* ___/___/___

Today I am *Grateful* for ______________________________

____

____

____

____

____

____

Joy always came after pain. - Guillaume Apollinaire

Day: ______________ *Date:* ___/___/___

Today I am *Grateful* for ______________________________

____

____

____

____

____

____

Day: ______________ *Date:* ___/___/___

Today I am *Grateful* for ______________________________

____

____

____

____

____

____

To be is to do. - Immanuel Kant

Day: ______________ *Date:* ___/___/___

Today I am *Grateful* for ______________________________

____

____

____

____

____

____

Day: ______________ *Date:* ___/___/___

Today I am *Grateful* for ______________________

Happiness never lays its finger on its pulse. - Adam Smith

Day: ______________ *Date:* ___/___/___

Today I am *Grateful* for ______________________

Made in the USA
Coppell, TX
11 December 2022